SHYAM BHATAWDEKAR
DR KALPANA BHATAWDEKAR

Essentials

of Effective

Communication

Essentials of Effective Communication

Books by Shyam Bhatawdekar and Dr Kalpana Bhatawdekar

Management, Business, Self-help and Personality Development Books

1. *HSoftware* (Human Software) (The Only Key to Higher Effectiveness)
2. Sensitive Stories of Corporate World (Management Case Studies)
3. Sensitive Stories of Corporate World (Volume 2) (Management Case Studies)
4. Classic Management Games, Exercises, Energizers and Icebreakers
5. Classic Management Games, Exercises, Energizers and Icebreakers (Volume 2)
6. Classic Team Building Games, Exercises, Energizers and Icebreakers
7. 101 Classic Management Games, Exercises, Energizers and Icebreakers
8. Stress? No Way!! (Handbook on Stress Management)
9. *HSoftware* (Shyam Bhatawdekar's Effectiveness Model)
10. Competency Management (Competency Matrix and Competencies)
11. Soft Skills You Can't Do Without (Goal Setting, Time Management, Assertiveness and Anger Management)
12. Essentials of Work Study (Method Study and Work Measurement)
13. Essentials of Time Management (Taking Control of Your Life)
14. Essentials of 5S Housekeeping
15. Essentials of Quality Circles
16. Essentials of Goal Setting
17. Essentials of Anger Management
18. Essentials of Assertive Behavior

19. Essentials of Performance Management and Performance Appraisal
20. Health Essentials (Health Is Wealth)
21. Essentials of Effective Communication
22. The Romance of Intimacy *(How to Enhance Intimacy in a Relationship?)*

Novels, Stories, Biographies and Travelogues

23. The Peace Crusaders *(Novel: how the peace crusaders established permanent peace on a war strewn planet?)*
24. Love Knows No Bounds *(Novel: a refreshingly different love story. Also available with the title "Good People")*
25. Funny (and Not So Funny) Short Stories
26. Stories Children Will Love (Volume 1: Bhanu-Shanu-Kaju-Biju and Dholu Ram Gadbad Singh)
27. My Father *(Biography)*
28. Travelogue: Scandinavia, Russia
29. Travelogue: Europe

To Our Family

Shyam Bhatawdekar   Dr Kalpana Bhatawdekar

"Communication" is one of the most important competencies every human being must continually improve in his various roles- individual, family person, social entity and professional. Every human being communicates a few hundred times or more everyday. Imagine its cumulative negative repercussions if he is not effective doing it. So if one wishes to benefit each time he communicates he has to be really good at it.

Therefore a thorough knowledge of "Effective Communication" becomes imperative. To facilitate gaining the knowledge in this vital subject in the shortest time, authors Shyam Bhatawdekar and Dr Kalpana Bhatawdekar included only the "essentials" of "Effective Communication" in the book.

The authors are topnotch business executives, successful entrepreneurs, highly sought after business and management consultants, eminent management gurus and scholars, authentic human behavior experts and prolific authors. And so the book becomes an authentic document on the subject.

To read more by the authors, refer their websites: http://shyam.bhatawdekar.com, *http://writings-of-shyam.blogspot.com* **and** http://management-universe.blogspot.com

Essentials of Effective Communication

Shyam Bhatawdekar
Dr Kalpana Bhatawdekar

Published by Publishing Division of

Prodcons Group

8, Pranjal Society, Shiv Tirth Nagar, Paud Road, Pune
411038 (India)

Email: prodcons@prodcons.com

For other web publications, refer: http://management-
universe.blogspot.com and
http://shyam.bhatawdekar.com

Contents

1. Introduction: Communication

Definitions

Communication is a pretty vast subject. No wonder many experts have defined it in many ways.

Goldhaber defines communication as "the process of creating and exchanging messages within a network of interdependent relationship to cope with the environmental uncertainty".

Keith Davis defines communication as "the transfer of information and understanding from one person to another person. It is a way of reaching others with facts, ideas, thoughts and values. It is a bridge of meaning among people so that they can share what they feel and know. By using this bridge a person can cross safely the river of misunderstanding that sometimes separates people."

Newman and Summer: a process of exchange of knowledge, ideas, thoughts, opinions, feelings, emotions or information between two or more individuals.

American Society of Training & Development (now, Association for Talent Development): a process of interchange of information to bring about a mutual understanding and confidence for good human relations.

Louis Allen: as a sum total of all the things one person does when he wants to create an understanding in the mind of another.

Katz and Kahn: as the exchange of information and transmission of meaning that is very essence of a social or organizational system.

We can gather from the above-mentioned definitions that communication is viewed as the transfer of information from one person to another, whether or not it elicits confidence. But the information transferred must be understandable to the receiver. It should never be forgotten that nothing could logically be called information unless it informs someone.

In its broadest sense, the purpose of communication in an enterprise or a society is to effect change- to influence action in the direction of enterprise and societal welfare.

Numerous Purposes

In everyday life, we use communication for many purposes listed below:

- Seeking or receiving information, giving information, allocating blame, encouragement, control, selling proposals, negotiating, confrontation.
- Talking to different levels within hierarchy- to individuals, to groups, to departments and externally to customers, suppliers, banks, other professionals.
- Using both formal communication: meetings, reports, proposals, notices; and informal communication: counseling, advising, talking to others.
- Working in different roles: as chairman, project leader, analyst, subordinate, colleague, member etc.
- Evaluating communications: are they facts, views, assumptions, perceptions, perspectives, gossip?
- Building networks to obtain real information.
- Trying to influence those over whom you have no power.

Again as mentioned earlier, in its broadest sense, the purpose of communication in enterprise and society is to effect change- to influence action in the direction of enterprise and social welfare.

Types of Communication

1. Verbal communication

- Oral
- Written

2. Non-verbal communication

- Silence
- Signals:
  - Audio signals
  - Visual signals

Communication Process

Communication is a process just like the other processes that consist of input, processor, output and feedback. In communication process the entities are:

- Sender (encoder): the one who sends a message
- Message (verbal and non-verbal): it has content-some data or information
- Medium (format): message is sent verbally or through other audio signals, in writing or visually
- Stimuli (noise): controllable and uncontrollable elements that disturb the real content being transmitted are psychological, environmental, physical and semantic
- Receiver (decoder): an entity that receives the message and interpretes it
- Feedback (verbal and non-verbal): receiver's response to the sender on receiving the message

Communication can take place between:

- one sender and one receiver
- one sender and many receivers
- many senders and one receiver
- many senders and many receivers

Communication can be face to face (physically or digitally or both together), over telephone(s), in writing (emails, e-chats, letters, memos, reports, notices, billboards etc), through audio-visual or audio means (audio clips, audio-visual presentations, movies etc).

For communication to be effective sender decides upon the objective(s) of his communication, accordingly drafts a suitable message, uses the most appropriate medium (media) to transmit the message, makes sure that the elements that might disturb the process of communication are eliminated or reduced to desirable minimum and ensures timely receipt of his message by the receiver. Receiver interpretes the message of the sender and may or may not send the feedback to the sender. For communication to be complete and effective the sender should try to elicit receiver's response and seek his feedback. He should also keep track to ensure that the intended objectives of the communication are achieved.

Check and Re-check Your Communication

To ensure high efficacy of communication one should check continuously, during the communication process, what the message really is and how it is being received by the receiver. For this, check it at each stage e.g. sending, receiving, understanding, accepting.

Checklist

Sender

- Who: To whom should the message go?
- Why: Why am I communicating? What is the objective of my communication? What are my motives?
- What: Decide what to communicate. Be clear about what you need to communicate.
- When: Choose the best time for optimum reception.
- How: Use language the receiver will understand and which is unambiguous.
- Where: Choose a location that will not interfere with the reception, understanding and acceptance of the message: Privately? Home or away? In a group? At work or outside?
- Keep checking with receiver.

Receiver

- Be fully attentive to sender.

- Understand actively the message being sent.
- Ask for clarification, repetition, where necessary.
- Keep checking with sender.

Together

- Realize that misunderstandings are bound to occur and be alert for all cues to this effect.
- Understand again.
- Test your understanding of the message.
- Share opinions, feelings and perceptions generated by the message.

2. Barriers and Distortions

Barriers to Communication

An effective communicator is aware of the following barriers to good communication. These barriers make the communication less effective i.e. the communication is not understood by the receiver the way it was meant to be understood.

- Communication aimed at eliciting from the receiver only the things the sender wants to hear thus sidelining or ignoring receiver's real views or needs.
- Tendency to send the information that reinforces sender's pre-existing views thus deliberately or unconsciously avoiding any or even important conflicting or contradictory information.
- Perceptions about the communicator by the audience affects the effectiveness of his messages. Personality, integrity, esteem and trust of the communicator as held or perceived in the

audience's mind impacts on the audience reaction or response.

- Words, jargons, sentences and expressions (verbal and non-verbal) mean different things to different people. If not chosen with due care may distort the communication and are likely to be misinterpreted by the receiver.

- Poorly or badly expressed messages may lack details, omit important content, present incoherent ideas, result in unstructured message etc.

- Message received from one person and being passed on to another person may suffer due to its faulty translation before it reaches the ultimate receiver.

- In relay of communication that crosses several persons in succession, a part of it may be lost during its repeated transmissions. Poor retention of the original message by each of the senders before being transmitted to the next-in-line receiver adds to this loss.

- Inattention or lack of attention of the receiver of the communication due to several factors is yet another barrier.

- Assumptions on certain aspects of a message made by the sender remain unclarified till the message is received by the receiver. In a way the receiver is taken for granted on that aspect of communication and finds a gap in communication.

- At times communication is intended to bring about some changes. The people involved in the change situation need adequate time to readjust themselves. Insufficient adjustment period may make the communication ineffective.

- Premature evaluation of a received message or about to be received message by the receiver without giving it the deserved consideration with an open mind poses a roadblock to communication.

- Non-verbal communication by body language, gestures or grunts is prone to several interpretations by different receivers based on their cultural backgrounds.

- Certain negative emotions such as anger, disgust, disappointment, sadness, frustration etc and at times, even the positive emotions like happiness, love, joy etc may create an emotional barrier in communication. Both the sender as well as the receiver may lose the clarity of the intended communication

- Communication or disclosure of some ideas and facts may instil a sense of fear or insecurity in the mind of the communicator. This may stop him from communicating freely and result in incomplete communication.

- Certain factors (laguage problems, physical disturbances, racial or cultural biases, emotional disturbance etc) pose distractions or interruptions in the smooth flow of communication or information. They are termed as noise. Any kind of noise is a barrier to communication.

- Little or no consideration on deciding an optimal size of a group being addressed may make your communication ineffective. Also little or no consideration on the size (chunkiness) of your message may also have an impact.

- Failure to communicate particularly when a non communication may pose criticality in the resultant situation is itself a barrier.

Overcoming these barriers is essential for effective communication.

Overcoming Barriers to Communication

One way of reducing the effects of these barriers is to check continuously during the communication process what the message really is and for this check it at each stage e.g. sending, receiving, understanding, accepting.

- Receiver is the most important entity in communication process. Therefore orient your communication to the world of the receiver.
- Make sure to receive feedback from the receiver(s) of your communication. Feedback is always very useful.
- Face-to-face communication can be more effective under most of the circumstances. Bank on it when appropriate.
- Use reinforcement to emphasize the vital aspects of your communication.
- Direct and simple language is far more effective than a flowery, roundabout and complicated language.
- Your communication will be more effective if your actions are in consonance with your words.

- Use of different channels of communication is better because if one channel does not work, the other channel(s) may.

- Reduce problems of size by replacing a chunky communication by short and sweet communication.

Distortions in Communication

This part of the chapter has been written in a lighter vein. Yet it underscores the horrible outcomes of an ineffective communication.

Given below are two hilarious pieces on distortions in communication. Though to be taken in a lighter vein, it can be vouched that such things do take place in real life. As such they amply warn the disasters of distortion in communication.

Examples of Distortions

Example 1:

1. Communication from Managing Director to Works Director:

Tomorrow morning there will be a total eclipse of the sun at nine o'clock. There is something which we cannot see happen everyday, so let the workforce line up outside in their best clothes to watch it. To mark the occasion of this rare occurrence I will personally explain it to them. If it is raining we shall not be able to see it very well and in that case the workforce should assemble in the canteen.

2. Communication as passed down from Works Director to General Works Manager:

By order of the managing director there will be a total eclipse of the sun at nine o'clock tomorrow morning. If it is raining we shall not be able to see it very well on the site, in our best clothes. In that case the disappearance of the sun will be followed through in the canteen. There is something that we cannot see happen everyday.

3. Communication as passed down from General Works Manager to Works Manager:

By the order of the managing director we shall follow through, in our best clothes, the disappearance of the sun in the canteen at nine o'clock tomorrow morning. The managing director will tell us whether it is going to rain. This is something which we cannot see happen everyday.

4. Communication as passed down from Works Manager to Foreman:

If it is raining in the canteen tomorrow morning, which is something that we cannot see happen everyday, our managing director, in his best clothes, will disappear at nine o'clock.

5. Communication as passed down from Foreman to Shop Floor:

Tomorrow morning at nine o'clock our managing director will disappear. It's pity that we cannot see this happen everyday.

Example 2:

A reporter from a news agency is interviewing Mr Malin Goody (the most prominent politician of the ruling party in one of the countries that has been constantly in news past few weeks): "Let me start our interview with the most important question hovering the minds of our citizens these days. And the question is- what is your most favorite fruit Mr Goody?"

Goody: "Mango."

Interviewer: "You said 'Mango' sir?"

Goody: "Yes."

Within a minute this exchange is carried by all TV news channels in the country as "breaking news" with the header, "Goody does not like guavas."

Spokespersons of different political parties/NGOs are invited to give their reaction.

Jit Avar (a political leader of the opposition in country's parliament): Our great Mahatma Gururaj used to like banana, which is easily available all across the country and cheap; so even the poor people can afford it. It is a fruit of common man. Goody is basically against Mahatma. So it is obvious that he does not like bananas. He represents Mathan who killed Mahatma Gururaj.

Manu Tari (another politician who represents minorities of the country): Goody does not like guava because of its green color! This shows his anti-minority bias! Shame on him!!

Abhi Malkan (a leader with socialistic inclination): Not surprised Goody likes an expensive fruit like mango. By that choice he is mocking the poor masses of our nation. He is against the poor of the country.

Papa Jose (a prominent leader who is a proponent of secularism): I am not like Goody who only likes specific things or items. My food intake is all-inclusive and I respect all foods like I respect all religions. I like yellow mangoes, green guavas and white amlas (a citrus fruit). Tomorrow I am going on a visit to the poor people of my electoral region living in poor huts where I will share and eat green and yellow skinned bananas with them.

Viji Viz (founder of a prominent non-profit NGO): Goody is a rotten mango and must therefore be immediately removed from the basket. Otherwise all mangoes in the basket will rot. A rotten mango like Goody has no place in the secular, all-inclusive basket of our great nation.

Nick Walia on country's most popular TV channel at its ten o'clock news: Welcome all! A new day and a new topic for discussion today. Goody has revealed his ugly, communal facade by declaring that he liked mangoes. By deliberately avoiding green guavas from the list of fruits he likes, Goody has clearly demonstrated his anti-minority, communal mentality. To debate this ultra important national topic we have among us Mr Raghav Bhan of the ruling party, Mr Salil Sahay of the principal opposition and great and original thinker Mr Madan Kare.

A comment by an independent elite of the country Deep Gaokar: "Goody likes mangoes a native fruit which mean he hates olives, the Italian fruit. This shows a narrow nationalism. He and his party's people have no international taste."

3. Body Language

Two Main Types of Communication

- Verbal communication: by speaking, writing using language etc.
- Non-verbal communication: by body postures, gestures, facial expressions, grunts (paralinguistics), tone of voice, eye contact and eye movements etc.

Body Language: Form of Non-verbal Communication

- Body postures, gestures, facial expressions, grunts (paralinguistics), tone of voice, eye contact and eye movements etc form the body language.
- Using this kind of body language, one can express or communicate.
- Body language can be used in conjunction with verbal message or without it.
- One could use a single body language cue or use in concert with other body language cue(s).
- Body language may provide cues regarding one's attitude or state of mind. It may indicate relaxed

state, pleasure, amusement, boredom, attentiveness, aggression, to quote a few of the cues.

Average Percentage of Body Language in Communication

Based on certain researches:

- Some people estimate it around 90% to 95%.
- Others estimate it at 60% to 70%.

It may not be wrong to conservatively estimate that at least some 50% of the meaning of any communication is understood from non-verbal cues or the body language. Even then it is pretty high percentage.

Therefore, understanding the body language for using it for one's own communication or in understanding others' communication is important.

If communication consists of 50% verbal and 50% non-verbal, the two together must be interpreted. At times the two components may be in harmony with each other (complementing each other) and at other times, the verbal communication may not be matched equally by the body language. It is important, then, to specifically interpret the body language.

Parts of the Body Language

You can send signals with individual parts of the body as well as in concert. Given below are the details of various parts of the body.

- Head: face, cheek, chin, mouth, lips, teeth, tongue, nose, eyes, eyebrow, forehead, hair.
- Arms: elbow, hand, finger.
- Torso: neck, shoulder, chest, back, belly, bottom, hips.
- Legs: thigh, knee, foot.

Body Language: Kinesics and Proxemics

Kinesics

- Facial expressions: Smile, frown, narrowed eyes, transmitting friendliness, anger.

- Gestures: Pointing fingers, thumbs up sign, shakes of the head, transmitting an emphasizing focus, congratulations or disagreements.
- Movements: Quick pacing up and down, finger drumming, leisurely strolling, transmitting impatience, boredom or relaxation.

Proxemics

- Physical contact: Shaking hands, prodding with forefinger, clapping on the back, transmitting greetings, insistence or friendship.
- Positioning: Keeping a respectful distance, looking over someone's shoulder, sitting close to someone, transmitting awareness of differing status, a close working relationship or relaxed mutual trust.
- Posture: Standing straight and erect, lounging, sitting hunched up, leaning forward, spreading oneself in a chair, transmitting alertness and care, self-confidence (or even over-confidence), nervousness.
- Paralinguistics: Feedback sounds of surprise or agreement, of annoyance or impatience- "uh-uh", "whew", "oops", "tsk", "tut-tut" etc.

Body Language Is Cultural

In different cultures people use different body language; it is not universal. Therefore, one should be careful in interpreting the body language.

In one culture, the meaning of a particular body language could be entirely different from the other culture. Therefore, people from different cultures can interpret body language in different ways.

Study of cultural differences vis-à-vis body language is useful.

Body Language Can be Deceptive in Case of Physically Challenged or Sick

Physically challenged people and people with certain specific disabilities (e.g. autistic, spastic) use and understand body language differently or not at all. Interpreting their gestures and facial expressions or lack of them within the framework of the usually understood body language may lead to incorrect meaning.

Examples: Body Language & Its Interpretation

- Generally, person crossing his arms across the chest can indicate that he is positioning an unconscious barrier between him and others. He is defensive.

- When situation is amicable, person crossing his arms across the chest can mean that he is thinking deeply about what is being discussed.

- But in a critical or confrontational situation, person crossing his arms across the chest can mean that he is expressing opposition, especially if he is leaning away.

- In addition to what is described in the earlier point, harsh or blank facial expression can indicate hostility.

- At times, crossed arms can be interpreted for submissiveness.

- Standing and rubbing hands together quickly can show anxiety.

- Standing and rubbing hands together slowly (in washing the hands motion) can state that I am through with it.

- Pulling right or left ear, putting finger inside the collar or pulling eyelid with finger can show disagreement with the other person.
- Speaking with palms upwards may mean open attitude or person is requesting help.
- Sitting at the desk, with elbows on the desk and hands being in steeple position looking like church tower with finger tips together can indicate keen listening.
- Seated, looking down with crossed legs may point to pensive mood.
- Hands on knees, leaning slightly forward and feet flat on the ground may indicate readiness or the person is about to respond.
- Palm on my face with one finger pointing toward ceiling can show that the person is immersed in deep thought.
- Hands supporting the chin and shoulders start to droop may be an indication of fatigue or feeling a bit depressed.
- Hands on hips may indicate impatience.
- Locking hands behind the back may indicate self-control.

- Locking hands behind head may indicate confidence.
- Sitting with a leg over the arm of the chair may be interpreted as indifference.
- Consistent eye contact can indicate that a person is thinking positively of what the speaker is saying.
- Consistent eye contact can also mean that the other person does not trust the speaker enough to take his eyes off the speaker.
- Lack of eye contact can indicate negativity.
- Persons with anxiety disorders are often unable to make eye contact without discomfort.
- If a person is looking at you but is giving the arms-across-chest cue, it can indicate that something is bothering the person and that he wants to talk about it.
- While making direct eye contact a person is fiddling with something, even while directly looking at you, it can indicate that his attention is elsewhere.
- When a person is not convinced by what someone is saying, his attention invariably wanders and the eyes will stare away for an extended period. Disbelief is often indicated by averted gaze or by touching the ear or scratching the chin.

- Person looking down and picking up imaginary bits off the suit or clothes when someone is speaking with him can mean boredom, not listening or snobbery.

- Boredom is also indicated by the head tilting to one side, or by the eyes looking straight at the speaker but becoming slightly unfocused.

- Interest can be indicated through posture or extended eye contact, such as standing and listening properly.

- Deceit or the act of withholding information can sometimes be indicated by touching the face during conversation.

- Excessive blinking is a well-known indicator of someone who is lying.

- Absence of blinking can also represent lying.

4. Written Communication

Types of Communication

1. Verbal communication

- Oral
- Written

2. Non-verbal communication

- Silence
- Signals:
  - Audio signals
  - Visual signals

Advantages of Written Communication

- Provides a permanent record and reference.
- Can be used as documentary evidence in cases of legal matters.
- Helps promotion of uniform policies and procedures.

- Can cover a large number of people in case of mass communication.
- Builds up an image for the organization.
- Helps in bringing in objectivity/clarity in allocation of responsibilities, performance appraisals, delegation, decision making etc.
- Avoids an effect on phonetics (science of sounds).

Disadvantages of Written Communication

- Creates enormous records that require lots of storage and retrieval.
- Does not evoke immediate feedback/response.
- More time consuming process- sending, receiving, results. Therefore, slower.
- Costly.
- Compared to non-verbal communication, somewhat impersonal.
- Semantics play an important role.

Tips on Improved Written Communication

- Write from the reader's viewpoint.
- Aim at specific objectives.

- Show reader/receiver the benefit(s).
- Choose words that draw pictures.
- Have action in your verbs.
- Avoid unnecessary jargons.
- Write short sentences- average maximum 20 words in a sentence.
- Use paragraphing.
- In longer written reports, use titles and sub-titles.
- Organize for interest and action.
- Contents of your written communication should be consistent with what you had said on the phone or in earlier correspondence.
- Develop your vocabulary.
- Simplify.

Double Check Your Written Communcation for

- Is your written communication complete in every respect?
- Have you checked the accuracy of facts and contents as well as grammar, punctuation etc?
- If there was any issue or problem for which you are writing, has it been brought out clearly?

- Have you clearly clarified the purpose of writing as to what you intend to achieve?
- Has your key message been appropriately and correctly included?
- Have you provided the supporting details in your communication?
- Is the organization of your written communication cohesive and sequential?
- Is the overall effect on the reader(s) right and as desired?

Checklist

Check your written communication against each of the following:

1. Preparing
2. Composing
3. Logical structuring
4. Formatting
5. Visual appeal
6. Grammar
7. Punctuation
8. Effective subject line

9. Salutation and signing off

10. Using simple words

11. Effective vocabulary

12. Avoiding jargon and cliche

13. Avoiding archaic phrases

14. Correct tone and attitude

15. Courtesy

16. Ethics

Business Correspondence

Protocol

Salutation:

Male recipient: Mr, Sir, Dr
Female recipient: Ms, Miss, Mrs, Dr, Madam
Company as recipient: Messrs, M/S

Complimentary close:

If addressed as Dear Sir: Yours faithfully, Cordially yours,
Yours sincerely

If addressed as Dear Mr Kulkarni: Yours sincerely, Sincerely

If addressed as Dear Rakesh/ Dear Anita: Sincerely, Yours sincerely

Other closing details: Office landline and cell phone numbers, office/correspondence address, your office hours/work days.

Effective Sentences

- No sentence should be more than 20 words long.
- In writing sentences, follow logical sequence: background or explanation of earlier events, then events or what happened next and finally, results or the conclusions.
- Writing in the active voice is simpler and makes more impact. Instead of writing "This defect can only be rectified by him", write, "Only he can rectify this defect".
- Use correct grammar.
- In writing business letters/emails you normally want your readers to do what you suggest. Construct sentences with this end in mind.

Paragraph Writing

You must follow three principles:

1. Unity: Every sentence in paragraph must be closely connected with the main topic of the paragraph. The paragraph and every part of it must be the expression of one theme or topic. Use a good "topic sentence" at the beginning of a paragraph. Then use supporting "specific details" to develop the topic sentence. For specific details give "additional information" related to that specific.

2. Order: Logical sequence of thought.

3. Variety: Avoid monotony by using different lengths of the paragraphs, using different sentence construction.

Also, write down events in the order they happened. The time line is a simple and effective method of organizing your writing.

5. Email Communication: Etiquette

Background

- Communication using emails has become very important and essential in professional as well as personal life.
- Communication using emails is prompt, direct and without disturbances.
- These days most of the persons prefer email communication over other forms of communication.
- Effectiveness and efficiency of email communication can be increased provided one develops the skills of communicating using emails.

Considering the above-mentioed aspects it is imperative to know in-depth the email etiquette. This will ensure that even inadvertently you do not commit those email mistakes which many commit because of their ignorance and lack of email skills.

Comprehensive List of Email Etiquette

- If you are employed by an organization, find out its email policy. Since the organization is providing you the resources, it can monitor how you should use those resources. It is a good idea to use work email account strictly for work or business related matters. Send and receive your private email communication by using your personal account.

- Make certain that you are writing the email to the right person.

- Plan out as to what you wish to achieve through your email; its objectives. The entire effectiveness of your email lies in the answer to question, "Did you ultimately achieve the objective for which you wrote the email?"

- Get all the contents, facts and figures at one place before you start writing your email. You may have to refer to other related correspondence and literature for this.

- Chalk out the complete contents of the email you wish to write, their sequence, paragraphing and flow for your email.

- Your email should also include the content (in the form of short sentences, questions, directives etc) that will elicit the desired response or action from the receiver.

- Rather than asking the receiver to recall an earlier message, include the earlier message in your email. Maintain the complete thread of correspondence on that particular subject matter.

- Give a short and yet, meaningful subject title. This is very important- give it a thought. It should not be too big or even too short. It should be specific and not vague. Subject title should give an idea of what the email is all about and provide a reason to the receiver to read it. These days people receive literally hundreds of emails everyday and may not have the time to open each of them. If you want the receiver of your email to give your email a priority or urgency, you should motivate him to do so by assigning your email an appropriate subject line.

- Be precise, concise and to the point. Get on with your key points of communication as quickly as possible.

- Use short sentences and paragraphs. However, do not allow the brevity to be mistaken for rudeness or to interfere with its comprehensiveness.
- Do not write very long emails (never longer than a page).
- In case you are sending an email reply, reply to all the points raised by the other person. Add anything that you want the other person to tell you and do for you.
- Send a prompt reply; that is the very reason you are using email.
- Use proper grammar, spellings and punctuation. Use the spell and grammar checks but do not blindly depend upon them for complete accuracy or correctness. Use also your native wisdom.
- Do not use all capital letters in your email; in email lingo it means you are shouting or screaming.
- Do not use all lower case letters too. Why flout the conventional way of writing English language?
- Emails are more informal as compared to the conventional letters but never be loose. Therefore, emails are more personal sort but yet businesslike.
- Use proper layout or format.
- Should look aesthetically appealing.

- Use "high priority (high importance)" option only if your email really deserves it.
- Use "request a delivery receipt" or "request a read receipt" option only when you think it is very important for you. Need not use it every time.
- Do not use "reply to all" unless you really wish to reply to all.
- Do not mark "Cc" or "Bcc" to those who are not connected with the business related to the subject matter.
- Before sending the message, double-check the list of recipients. Also, in case of multiple people with similar names in the address book, be careful to choose the right person.
- Do not attach the attachments that are not necessary. Attach only the essential attachments to your email (and make their mention in your email). You must have experienced the frustration of receiving large and unwanted attachments or unsolicited files. Therefore, in sending out the emails to others, do so only if absolutely necessary.
- Do not use abbreviations (unless they are absolutely universally understood) or emotions.
- Do not use slang in your use of language.

- Do not use email for confidential matters or matters of secret nature. Discuss the confidential matters with others in face to face communication or exceptionally, over phone.
- Use active voice, avoid using passive voice.
- Do not use lengthy or long winding sentences. Use short sentences (maximum 15 to 20 words in a sentence).
- Do not forward all kinds of emails to anyone and everyone.
- Do not write or forward emails containing defamatory, derogatory, unfounded, loose, ethnic, racist and obscene remarks.
- Do not forward chain emails.
- Do not forward the jokes all over the place.
- Do not forward virus hoaxes.
- Draft your email messages with an understanding and assumption that they could be deliberately or inadvertently get forwarded by some receiver(s) to other people whom the email was not intended to be sent. So always be careful about what and how you write. The contents of your email therefore should not include offensive or abusive or obscene

language or should not include confidential or secret information.

- If you are a receiver of an email and if you notice that the email has also been wrongly forwarded to a person who you are sure will get offended by that email, you may alert the sender about it to save the embarrassment both to the sender and to that particular receiver. Perhaps the sender may recall that email.

- One need not read the recalled message since the sender has sent that message wrongly and he does not want a wrong message to be acted upon.

- Never reply to spam. It may be dangerous security wise.

- Add disclaimers in your email as appropriate.

- When unhappy with an email or email reply from others, do not use a number of exclamations or question marks in your reply email to tell the recipient so.

- If you are annoyed with a colleague or client, do not send a curt, cold or rude email.

- Do not point out spelling errors and grammatical mistakes to senders of emails to you.

- Do you ever get into arguments in emails and send copies of the verbal "match" to everyone? If you do, stop it.

- Do not give email ids of other persons to anyone without taking their permission.

- Check your email thoroughly for contents, facts and figures, grammar, spellings etc once again before dispatching it. Make sure that you have spelt out the name(s) of the receiver(s) correctly.

- Always conclude every email by writing your name, address, phone number and your email address. This way, recipients get the information on multiple means of contacting you in case they do not wish to communicate with you only through emails and wish to use other means. This information is also useful to the people to whom your email might be forwarded.

- Communication through email is very efficient way of communicating and should be used. However, if your native wisdom suggests that calling the other person or speaking with him in person is more appropriate and you should not send an email, do so. Or some situations may warrant both types of communication.

- Never hack into any one's email.

Checklist

Check your email communication against each of the following:

1. Preparing
2. Composing
3. Logical structuring
4. Formatting
5. Visual appeal
6. Grammar
7. Punctuation
8. Effective subject line
9. Salutation and signing off
10. Using simple words
11. Effective vocabulary
12. Avoiding jargon and cliche
13. Avoiding archaic phrases
14. Correct tone and attitude
15. Courtesy
16. Ethics

6. Email Communication: Ready Reckoner

Given below are the ready-to-use phrases that you can safely use in your written communication, particularly in your email communication without having to spend your time in thinking about what and how to write in a specific situation or setting. The typical phrases that can be used are given for formal as well as informal email communication.

The ready reckoner of the email phrases pertains to following types of email communication:

- Basics of email communication
- Email communication for arranging meetings
- Email communication on invitations
- Email communication on business deals/projects
- Email communication on seeking/giving clarifications

Given below are the typical phrases that you can readily use in each of the above-mentioned situations. However, if you are confident to do better than this, feel free to do so.

1. Basics of Email Communication

Addressing

Formal setting

Dear Mr/Ms/Mrs Mathews

Informal setting

Hi/Hello Alice, Daniel, (or no name at all)

Previous Referencing

Formal setting

Thank you for your email of ....

Further to your last email, ...

I apologize for not getting in touch with you before.

Informal setting

Thanks for your email.

Re your email, ...

Sorry I haven't written for ages, but I've been really busy.

Purpose

Formal setting

I am writing in connection with ....

I am writing with regard to ....

In reply to your email, here are ....

Your name was given to me by ....

We would like to point out that ....

The purpose of my email is ....

Informal setting

Just a short note about ....

I'm writing about ....

Here's the .... you wanted.

I got your name from ....

Please note that ....

My purpose to write is ....

Furnishing Information

Formal setting

I'm writing to let you know that ....

We are able to confirm that ....

I am delighted to tell you that ....

We regret to inform you that ....

Informal setting

Just a note to say ....

We can confirm that ....

Good news!

Unfortunately, ...

Attachment(s) to Email

Formal setting

Attached is my report.

I'm sending you .... as a PDF file.

Informal setting

I've attached ....

Here is the .... you wanted.

Seeking Information

Formal setting

Could you give me some information about ....?

I would like to know ....

I'm interested in receiving/finding out ....

Informal setting

Can you tell me a little more about ....?

I'd like to know ....

Please send me ....

Other Requests

Formal setting

I'd be grateful if you could ....

I wonder if you could ....

Do you think I could have ....?

Thank you in advance for your help in this matter.

Informal setting

Please could you ....

Could you ....?

Can I have ....?

I'd appreciate your help on this.

Promising Action

Formal setting

I will ....

I'll investigate the matter.

I will contact you again shortly.

Informal setting

I'll ....

I'll look into it.

I'll revert to you soon.

Offering Help

Formal setting

Would you like me to ....?

If you wish, I would be happy to ....

Let me know whether you would like me to ....

Informal setting

Do you want me to ....?

Shall I ....?

Let me know if you'd like me to ....

Concluding Comments

Formal setting

Thank you for your help.

Do not hesitate to contact us again if you require any further information.

Please feel free to contact me if you have any questions. My direct line is ....

Informal setting

Thanks again for ....

Let me know if you need anything else.

Just give me a call if you have any questions. My number is ....

Close

Formal setting

I'm looking forward to ....

Give my regards to ....

Best wishes

Regards

Informal setting

Looking forward to ....

Best wishes to ….

Speak to/See you soon.

Bye (for now)/All the best

2. Email Communication for Arranging Meetings

Purpose of Communication

Formal setting

I'm writing to arrange a time for our meeting.

What time would be convenient for you?

Informal setting

Just a quick note to arrange a time to meet.

When would suit you?

Venue and Time of Meeting

Formal setting

Could we meet on (day) in the (morning) at (time)?

Informal setting

How about (day) at (time)?

Are you free sometime next week?

My Availability

Formal setting

I would be able to attend the meeting on Wednesday morning.

I'm out of the office until 2pm. Any time after that would be fine.

I'm afraid I can't manage next Tuesday.

Informal setting

I'm free Wednesday ....am.

I won't be around until after lunch. Any time after that is okay.

Sorry, can't make it next Monday.

Confirmation

Formal setting

I'd like to confirm ....

That's fine. I will call/email you tomorrow to confirm the details.

Wednesday is good for me.

That should be okay. I'll revert to you if there's a problem.

Request for Reschedule

Formal setting

This is to let you know that I will not be able to attend the next meeting next Thursday. I wonder if we could move it to ....? I apologize for any inconvenience caused.

Informal setting

Re our meeting next week, I'm afraid I can't make Thursday. How about .... instead? Sorry for the inconvenience.

Close

Formal setting

I look forward to meeting you in Mumbai. Let me know if you need to change the arrangements.

Informal setting

See you in Mumbai. Give me a call if anything changes.

3. Email Communication on Invitations

Sending an Invite

Formal setting

We would be very pleased if you could come to ....

I would like to invite you to .... /to attend our ....

Please let me know if you will be able to attend.

Informal setting

I'm writing to invite you to ....

Would you like to come to ....?

Please let me know if you can make it.

Preparation

Formal setting

Before the meeting it would be useful if you could prepare ....

It would be helpful if you could bring ....

Informal setting

Please prepare .... before the meeting.

Please bring to the meeting ....

Acceptance

Formal setting

Thank you for your kind invitation.

The date you suggest is fine.

I would be delighted to attend the meeting. I am sure it will be very useful.

Informal setting

Thanks a lot for the invitation.

The date's fine for me.

Regret

Formal setting

Thank you for your kind invitation. Unfortunately, I have another appointment on that day. Please accept my apologies. I hope we will have the opportunity to meet on another occasion in the near future. I am sure that the meeting will be a great success.

Informal setting

Thanks a lot for your kind invitation. Unfortunately, I have something else in my schedule on that day. I hope we can meet up soon. Good luck with the meeting!

4. Email Communication on Business Deals/Projects

Seeking Information

What are your usual charges (fees/rates) for ....?

Can you give me some more information about ....?

Requests

Do you think you could ....?

Would you be able to ....?

Highlighting a Point

My main concern at this stage is ....

The main thing for me is ....

Inviting Suggestion(s)

How do you think we should deal with this?

What do you think is the best way forward?

Making Suggestion(s)

Why don't you ....?

What about if we ....?

Being Firm while Negotiating

I understand what you're saying about .... (but ....)

I can see what you're saying, (but ....)

Displaying Flexibility

We would be prepared to .... (if ....)

I am willing to .... (if ....)

Agreement

Okay, I'm happy with that for now.

That's fine.

Next Action(s)

I'll be in touch again soon with more details.

Let's talk next week and see how things are going.

Close

I look forward to working with you.

I'm sorry that we couldn't use your services this time, but I hope there will be another opportunity.

5. Email Communication on Seeking/Giving Clarifications

Concerning Faulty Email Transmits

Did you get my last message sent on ....?
Sorry, you forgot to attach the file. Can you send it again?

I got your email, but I can't open the attachment.

Did you mean to send it? I don't want to open it in case it has a virus.

Seeking Clarifications

I'm not sure what you meant by ....? Could you clarify?

Which .... do you mean?

I don't understand this point. Can you explain in detail?

Are you sure about that?

Giving Clarifications

Sorry, what I meant was ..., not ....

I thought ...., but I may be wrong.

I'll check and get back to you.

The correct information is given below. Please amend your records accordingly.

Sorry, forget my last email. You're right.

Close

I hope this clarifies the situation.

Get back to me if there's anything else.

7. Public Speaking

Finer Points of Public Speaking

- Decide on date, time and city/town of your speech.
- Decide on the length of your speech i.e. the duration for which you will speak.
- Know your audience well in advance of the actual day of your speech.
- Find out what your audience expects from your speech? What are their needs?
- Choose an appropriate topic or subject accordingly.
- Give your speech a catchy title.
- Do good amount of research on the subject and collect authentic and correct information and data. Work out on issues and solutions pertaining to the topic.
- Preferably write down the entire speech. Keep the length of the write-up to fit into the time duration of your speech.
- Convert the speech into many points and make cue cards. Note down one point on one cue card.

Arrange all the cue cards in a sequence and give them the serial numbers.

- Decide on the time you will like to give to each point. Write down the minutes you will take to elaborate the point on the respective cue card.
- Rehearse your speech.
- Sleep well on the night before the day of your speech. Look fully rested.
- Look your best on the day of your speech. Good overall grooming is very important.
- Look energetic and enthusiastic all the way.
- Shave (meant only for man).
- You should not smell. Hair should be done tastefully. Nails should be cut. Wash your mouth with a good mouth wash.
- Dress appropriately for the occasion. Don't wear casuals and also, don't overdress.
- Clothes should be clean, neat and well pressed (wrinkle free).
- Clothes should be decent fitting types.
- Dress should not be loud and gaudy.
- Wear a fresh pair of socks and shoes should be polished.

- Reach the venue ahead of time and make sure that the arrangements are as you desired them to be.
- Make sure that the microphone and loud speakers are working in case you are going to use them.
- If you wish to refer to any video projection during your speech, make sure that the equipment to do so is working.
- Present yourself as a confident person as you start your speech.
- Believe in yourself. Believe in what you are saying in your speech. Your listeners will tend to believe you that much more.
- People have come to listen to you because you are an authority on the topic. So behave like one. Don't feel shy or apologetic.
- Connect to your audience. Let them feel involved. Keep a good level of eye contact with the persons in your audience.
- Make the listeners feel that they are the center of attention (and not you).
- The language of your speech should be the language the audience understands. Do not use unnecessary jargon. If you have to use any jargon, explain its meaning in a simple to understand language.

- Use correct pronunciation and grammar.

- For your speech to make the audience spellbound by it, like a piece of music, it should have variety of notes, modulations, tempo, volume level etc. A monotonous speech is sure to make even the most interested listeners to fall asleep.

- Right kinds and right timings of pauses and instants of silence, loudness, softness and whispers, fast and slow tempo etc make the main points of your speech stand out and later on, these points are retained and make the desired impressions on the minds of the audience.

- You may read out the written speech. But since, normally it is difficult to memorize the entire speech, one has tendency to get their eyes glued to the written speech rather than making eye contacts with the audience and connecting with them.

- Therefore, preferably, more effective way is to use the points written on a paper or on the cue cards and elaborate on them in your own words and style rather than just reading out the written speech.

- While focusing attention on your audience, make sure that you run your eyes from left to middle to right and then, from right to middle to left and also, from front to back and from back to front. Don't focus just on one or two persons.

- Always address the audience while speaking and do not address an inanimate object like the ceiling or piece of furniture and distant tree or building.

- Do not keep pacing or move too much on the stage or the floor and do not keep on dancing on your feet or lean too much on the podium or the table.

- Use pleasant hand movements, facial expressions and gestures and other aspects of body language.

- Display good sense of humor while delivering your speech. However, never use the adult jokes or toilet humor in public. They are not in good taste.

- Apologize if you make a mistake in speaking. Humility is generally appreciated.

- All in all, design and deliver your speech such that it leaves an imprint. It should impact and inspire the listeners such that they start pondering over what you have spoken and even take actions to implement the points made out in your speech.

8. Presentation Skills

Purposes of Presentations (Partial List)

- For public address on any subject
- For debates in parliament
- For company meetings
- For outlining strategies
- For presenting business plans
- For presenting marketing plans
- For selling goods, services, concepts and ideas
- For presenting financial status
- For presenting project status
- For training programs and workshops
- For giving keynote address in professional conferences
- For employee induction
- For presentation about a company profile

Three Keys for Successful Presentations

- Overcoming nervousness
- Thorough preparation

- Good delivery

Overcoming Nervousness

- Know your subject
- Know your audience
- Know your objective
- Prepare
- Rehearse/Practice
- Practice
- Practice
- Practice (about practice, read later on this page. Also read articles "Life Management: Competencies" at *http://shyam-bhatawdekar.blogspot.com/*

Preparation

- Checking if I am competent to talk on the subject?
- Agreeing to make a presentation, agreeing to talk
- Getting informed on purpose of talk, schedule, audience profile and size, venue
- Zeroing in on the objectives
- Deciding what to say
- Structuring your talk

- Prepare your notes
- Prepare visual aids
- Rehearse
- Check and prepare arrangements on site

Structuring a Presentation

1. Prepare overall design: opening, body and wrap-up
2. Introduction and objectives, reasons for presentation: 10% of the time available.
3. Introduction of main themes, issues: 20% of the time available.
4. Development of main themes, issues: 40% of the time available.
5. Integration of main themes, issues: 20% of the time available.
6. Summary or conclusion: 10% of the time available.

You may like to keep aside some time for questions and answers. Announce it at the start of the talk.

Practice

- Reading through the material for your talk several times.

- Practicing in front of a mirror or using your friends as guinea pigs, if you feel the need.
- Assisting another person on a particular topic before presenting it yourself.
- Run through the entire talk. Don't just stop where you run into problems.

Also read articles "Life Management: Competencies" at *http://shyam-bhatawdekar.blogspot.com/*

Delivery

- Technique
- Manner

Profile of a Presenter

- Authentic
- Enthusiastic
- Confident
- Well mannered
- Well groomed (check for personal neatness; cleanliness; hair; nails; clothes- color, fashion, design, cut; accessories- shoes, belt, pen, spectacles, watch, jewelery; bad breath; body odor etc)

- Excellent presenter
- Excellent communication skills (verbal and non-verbal- body language)
- Excellent interpersonal skills
- High emotional intelligence in addition to high IQ
- Time conscious
- Action oriented
- Can relate to as to how his presentation will benefit the audience

Some Tips on Presentation Slides

- If a visual does not explain something better than words, do not use it.
- 5 minutes per slide- ballpark.
- One main idea with 5-9 points per slide.
- 5-7 words or say, around not more than 25 characters per point (talking points, not whole presentation- only highlights).
- Use graphics when they add to or help explain material.
- Don't overuse graphics.
- Use special effects if they help in improving the presentation quality.

- Do not overuse special effects.
- Any decent font.
- Large and bold enough to be seen on a big screen by the person sitting in the last row.

Some Tips on Opening a Talk or Presentation

An effective opening of presentation is half the battle won. It must aim to seek audience attention and interest. Different presenters try different things at different occasions to achieve this. Some of them are:

- Bringing the audience to the crossroads and then presenting your solutions.
- Presenting current startling facts in an authentic style.
- Highlighting the urgency of the situation.
- Interesting anecdote or story.
- Creating suspense.
- Humorous story.
- Presenting posers or questions to audience.
- Interesting authentic history on the topic.
- Painting future scenarios.

- Presenting the highlights of benefits of your talk to the audience.

Physical Setting of Venue of Presentation

- Appropriate.
- Good in size and shape to accommodate the number in audience.
- Will the people in the back be able to see?
- Comfortable.
- Flexible.
- Neat and clean.
- Not cluttered.
- Well ventilated.
- Well lighted.
- Acoustically effective.
- Has noise control.
- If familiar- it's bonus.
- Effective and comfortable seating arrangement and seating layout.
- Presentation gadgets and materials available, placed at convenient locations and in working condition.
- Restroom/bathroom conveniently located, nearby.

Effective Communication in Meetings

Face to face meetings, audio/telephone conferencing, video conferencing, web conferencing etc are quite in vogue in addition to the other methods of communication. Meetings are often used to:

- Inform and to clarify
- Exchange information
- Collect feedback
- Brainstorm ideas and solutions
- Make decisions
- Plan
- Workout implementation strategies
- Collaborate and strengthen teams

etc.

To make the meetings more effective one of the most important indredients of the meetings is effective communication by its members and chairperson.

One can use the following tips for effective communication in a meeting:

- Listen carefully to what the chairperson and other members are saying. Observe speaker's body language too.

- When a person is talking do not interrup him. After he has finished talking, take your turn to speak out. Make sure to enter into the discussion and present your viewpoint.

- Even if you do not agree to a point made by someone else in the meeting, treat him with decorum. Then present your opposing viewpoint assertively and politely.

- Put forth your ideas clearly, precisely and concisely. Do not waste the time of the meeting by lengthy and meaningless communication.

- Support your presentation or arguments with statistics, facts and figures. This is more important when you face difficult to convince people in the meeting.

- Stick to the agenda of the meeting.

- Monitor and control the communication to fit into the prescribed duration of the meeting.

- Facilitate others in the meeting to arrive at the desired outcomes of the meeting. Therefore steer the discussion to focus on the agenda item(s).

- If you are the chairperson of the meeting, circulate the minutes of the meeting to the attendees as well as to other concerned persons. Assign the accountabilities and deadlines clealy.

9. Listening

Listening Skill: an Important Skill to Understand Others and to Respond

- Listening is an important human skill.
- It is a subset of communication skills.
- Every interaction with others as well as self (introspection) involves some degree of listening.
- Listening strengthens the quality of communication, interpersonal relations, human relations, emotional intelligence, conflict management and team management.
- Every interaction requires one to respond and quality of listening improves the quality of response.

Hierarchy of Listening

There are two major types of listening:

1. Listening within the sphere of one's own HSoftware (overall mental frame consisting of values, knowledge, paradigms and will to act). This

type of listening is supportive of making the listener react, reply, control or manipulate the other person but not necessarily to understand the other person properly to respond or act in the best possible way. For more explanation of HSoftware, refer: *http://shyam.bhatawdekar.com*

2. Listening within the sphere of other's HSoftware (overall mental frame). Here the listening is done to understand the other person and not just to react, reply, control or manipulate the other person. By understanding the other person properly, the listener can respond or act in the best possible manner.

In turn, there are five levels of listening within the sphere of one's own HSoftware (overall mental frame):

1. Ignoring/showing indifference
2. Pretend listening
3. Selective listening
4. Patronizing listening
5. Attentive listening
6. Active listening

and one level of listening within the sphere of other's HSoftware (overall mental frame):

1. Empathic listening

It is also called empathetic listening.

Ignoring/Showing Indifference

- This is not listening at all. This happens when one person ignores the other person or shows indifference to what the other person is saying.
- This is pretty insulting to the other person.

Pretend Listening

- This happens when one person is making other person believe that he is listening though in reality, he is not listening.
- There may be several reasons to do so and the person may choose one or more reasons to ignore or be indifferent.
- The reason may also be that the person lacks the listening skills.

Selective Listening

- This happens when one listens to only selective portion of what the other person is saying.
- There may be several reasons to do so and the person may choose one or more reasons to use selective listening.
- The reason may also be that the person lacks in the listening skills.

Patronizing Listening

- This happens when the listener takes a patronizing position with reference to the other person.
- The person listens with a superior attitude; the superiority is drawn from power position, age, hierarchy, money etc.
- The person listens with an explicit or implicit posture to distribute favor or punishment to the other person.

Attentive Listening

- This happens when the person is really focusing on what the other person is saying and paying attention and understanding/trying to understand what the other person is saying.

- This is definitely a better form of listening but most of the times, the understanding of what the other person is saying will be influenced by the listener's own HSoftware (overall mental frame). His understanding may be erroneous.
- Here also, listening skill is not of the highest proficiency level.

Active Listening

- This happens when the listener tries to understand what the other person is saying by being interactive with him by giving him the feedback of his understanding.
- The feedback pertains more at the verbal level exchange of communication between the two.
- This is done through repeating or paraphrasing of understanding by the listener and transmitting that feedback to the other person for confirmation.

Empathic Listening

- This is the most effective level of listening.

- As mentioned earlier, listening is not done just to react, reply, control or manipulate the other person or the situation but to understand the other person properly to respond or act in the best possible way.
- The listener takes his time to diagnose.
- He tries first to understand, then, takes action to be understood.
- The listener puts himself in other person's shoes. The first step to put yourself in other's shoes is to first take out one's own shoes (keep your own HSoftware at bay to start with).
- Empathic listening is not technique oriented where as the other types of listening have techniques at their base to develop those listening skills.
- It is value based. It is based on respect for the other person as well as on openness and trust.
- The listener has to open an emotional bank account in the other person and that's how the person opens up.
- Listening has to be done with demonstrated intent to understand the other person.
- The listener should try to understand the other person fully and deeply, intellectually as well as emotionally. It does not necessarily mean that you

fully agree with him. Refer: *http://emotional-quotient-intelligence.blogspot.com/ (Emotional Intelligence)*

- Empathy is not sympathy. In sympathy you make other person dependent on you. Here you don't.

- Only 10% of our communication is by the words we say, another 30% is by our sounds and 60% by our body language. In empathic listening, the listener listens with his ears but also with his eyes and with his heart. One should listen for feeling and meaning.

- Empathic listening is the key to making deposits in emotional bank accounts of others.

- Apart from the basic need for physical survival, another basic need of human being is psychological survival- one wants to be understood and appreciated by others; one wants their affirmation and validation. Empathic listening satisfies this need.

- After this need is satisfied, one can then focus on influencing or problem solving.

10. Transaction Analysis

Knowledge and practice of "transaction analysis" goes a long way in communicating effectively. Transaction analysis is a vast topic. Yet its essential aspects that are presented here should give the readers a pretty good idea of what it is and how to use it for effective communication.

Major Areas of Transaction Analysis (TA)

- Ego states
- Transactions
- Life Positions
- Games
- Psychological Strokes

1. Ego States

Within each individual lie three ego states:

- Parent: a taught concept of life
- Adult: a thought concept of life
- Child: a felt concept of life

Parent

- Critical parent or controlling parent: setting standards, using authority, taking responsibility, being judgmental, exercising control
- Nurturing parent or loving parent: loving, nurturing, caring

Adult

- No subdivision
- Behavior of adult ego state: logical or rational, objective in assessment or evaluation, operates with the reality of here and now, thinks without bias or subjectivity

Child

- Free child: feelings and expressions of joy and happiness, spontaneous feelings, spontaneous actions without holding feelings
- Little professor (subset of free child): seat of intuition, genuine curiosity, creativity, bit of manipulation
- Adapted child: self control, compliance, politeness

- Rebellious child (subset of adapted child): rebelliousness

2. Transactions

Knowledge of ego states helps you to understand which way the communication is moving. Your own positioning in terms of your ego state and from which ego state the other person with whom you are communicating is responding will decide the outcome of communication.

- If both the parties in communication (or at least the one who has the knowledge and skill of ego states) adjust on appropriate ego states, the communication will result in a complementary transaction *or* complementary communication. Both the persons will feel satisfied with the conversation or communication. This enhances the interpersonal relationship. Refer*: http://interpersonal-relations.blogspot.com/ (Interpersonal Relations) and http://manage-conflict.blogspot.com/ (Conflict Management)*
- However, if they are not aware of this phenomena (of ego states), they are likely to end up in a cross

transaction or cross communication. They may get into a conflicting situation and communication will be cutoff. This will cause disruption in interpersonal relationships.

- At times the communication seems going on smoothly on the surface but actually it is a cross transaction for all the practical purpose. In such transactions the ego states complement each other at the social level but at the psychological level the contradiction takes place. This type of communication is called "ulterior transaction" or "ulterior communication". Ulterior transactions lead to playing "games" with each other. With games, there is an undercurrent of one-upmanship, exploitation and humiliation and this may jar the interpersonal relations.

3. Life Positions

At any point of time a person can be in one of the four types of life positions given below. The life positions of communicators influence and shape up communication. For more details on life position, refer: *(Life Positions and OKness)* http://life-positions.blogspot.com/

- I am OK, you are OK: A person accepts others in spite of their shortcomings and feels OK about himself despite not being perfect.
- I am OK, you are not OK: Comes over as distrustful, arrogant superior. Thinks that others are inferiors.
- I am not OK, you are OK: Recognized by attitudes of depression, powerlessness and inferiority. Thinks that others are better.
- A am not OK, you are not OK: A position of thorough hopelessness and despair

Obviously, I am OK, you are OK life position is the most healthy life position. A person in this life position will communicate more effectively.

4. Psychological Games People Play

- These are those seemingly straight transactions and conversations that have some underlying ulterior motive.
- Psychological games cause discomfort and bad feelings.

- When played to a higher/extreme degree, games culminate in very harmful and destructive behavior.
- Most people spend large proportion of their time and energy, playing games with others as adult part (ego state) of their personality are usually unaware of what is happening and they continue with games.
- One more reason for playing games is to confirm to a basic life position (OKness) described earlier.

We give below some of these games, the ones that are particularly played in an organization's environment or in any social setup.

Blemish: It is played to enjoy superior feelings. The person playing this game will find a minute fault (blemish) in other person's behavior or performance despite the fact that the job has been overall done well. The initiator of the game will open his comments with, "It's OK, you finally did well, but...."

Now I've got you: The person playing this game will set up or dig out a situation where the other person made some mistake, only to step in at a later stage to point out that mistake, with superior posture and smile of triumph.

Mine's better than yours: In this game the initiator consistently uses superlatives that show him in a superior position over the others. The usual expressions are, "I always stay in five start hotels when on holidays". "I was ill but it wasn't as bad as Mr XYZ". "My children go to the best school in the town" etc.

Why don't you, yes but: The initiator of the game invites suggestions or ideas from others in a meeting or in day-to-day encounters and when idea is given with, "Why not try this method...." the person playing this game always finds an objection by saying, "Yes, but, will it work or yes, but did you consider the high costs involved" etc. The suggestion howsoever good it may be is always played down with, "Yes, but...."

I was only trying to help you out: In this the game, the game player is usually behaving from his nurturing parent ego state. He will offer probably unsolicited advices to others time and again and due to this if his advice is rejected or not heeded to, he will say, "I was only trying to help you out" blaming the other person for not taking the advice in the right spirit.

Stupid: This person constantly misunderstands the directives or instructions given to him and keeps convincing himself that he is not intelligent enough to understand them properly as others do. It confirms his "I am not OK, others are OK" life position. And many a time, he may actually say, "I must be stupid".

Kick me: This person will provoke criticism from others and keeps making mistakes and keeps getting negative strokes from others. He is out to confirm his "Non OKness".

5. Psychological Strokes

Appropriate inclusion of psychological strokes in communication enhances the effectiveness of communication. Since psychological strokes play a great part in motivating the person(s) being communicated to, detailed knowledge of strokes is very important.

Recognition, Praise or Appreciation: *Basic for Human Motivation*

- We always face the challenge of motivating others- our children, students, workers, subordinates, colleagues, bosses, service providers, customers and list can go on.

- We also face the challenge of motivating self all the time.

- Lots of motivational theories are discussed and debated for their superiority and application but there is a very simple theory of motivation i.e. giving recognition and praising or appreciating others as well as self (or receiving praise for self). Refer: *(Motivation)* *http://motivation-people.blogspot.com/*

- Praising or appreciating is called giving "positive strokes" in applied psychology or in the discipline of transaction analysis (TA). Refer: *(Transaction Analysis-* *TA)* *http://transaction-analysis.blogspot.com/*

- Appreciating or praising people is a basic technique and yet, very effective in motivating anyone, from a pauper to a king. Who does not need praise, tell me.

Why the Need for Praise?

In order for babies to survive and grow, physically, mentally and emotionally, they need to be touched, fondled and shown recognition. This physical handling stimulates the release of growth hormones from the pituitary gland.

- Individuals deprived of such recognition and touch have been seen to be physically, mentally and emotionally retarded, at times so severely that death results.
- As one grows out of the childhood, while the important need for physical stimulus decreases, basic need for other forms of recognition stays. This need stays with everyone throughout his life.
- Inadequate recognition of the existence of the self often leads to mental anxiety, depression and illness.
- The fact is all of us need to be seen and recognized by others.
- To be starved of human contact and recognition is as bad as being starved of food.
- In terms of this need for positive strokes, we can be compared with the pets. As our dogs and cats need to be stroked for providing them our affection and attention, so it is also with us human beings. We also need to be "stroked" to recognize our existence. It is then called "psychological strokes".

- Psychological stroke is a unit of recognition.

Range of Strokes

- Strokes range from a casual nod to an intimate relationship.
- Some forms of recognition have a negative impact on the recipients and result in mild discomfort or even intense bad feelings.
- Other forms of recognition can have an effect on the recipient that can be described as ranging from no effect or neutral effect to intense pleasure.
- Recognition at times is given spontaneously with no conditions or strings attached to it. This is "unconditional recognition". For example, a mother showers her affection on her baby just for no reason; it is done absolutely unconditionally.
- Other form of recognition is "conditional". It is given subject to the fulfillment of some condition; for example, on accomplishment (or non-accomplishment) of some expected work or task. So, normally, conditional strokes are task related.

Use appropriate stroke in communication from this range.

Classification or Types of Strokes

Based on the range of strokes, described earlier, the psychological strokes are classified into following five categories.

1. Positive conditional stroke.
2. Positive unconditional stroke.
3. Negative conditional stroke.
4. Negative unconditional stroke.
5. Neutral or indifferent stroke.

We will describe each type of these strokes in some detail below.

Positive conditional stroke

- Here the person is appreciated or praised for having done or achieved something in an acceptable way.
- There is condition: if you do well I will appreciate otherwise not.
- So, having fulfilled a condition, if one is appreciated, he is receiving conditional positive stroke.
- Person is thus appreciated for doing.

Positive unconditional stroke

Here the person is appreciated without any condition. To receive the praise, fulfilling any condition is not necessary.

- Person is appreciated for being and not necessarily for doing.
- Parents love their children unconditionally most of the times. Or a boss is all praise for his favorite subordinate.

Negative conditional stroke

- Person is reprimanded or scolded or criticized for not fulfilling a condition in an acceptable manner.
- Typical rebuff will be: you have not done it the way it should have been done. It needs correction or rectification. Therefore, I am critical of it and you do not deserve my praise.

Negative unconditional stroke

- If a person gets rebuked or criticized for no rhyme or reason, he is receiving negative unconditional stroke.

- This stroke is also not for doing but for being a person who gets criticized by someone else. The person giving this stroke just happens to dislike the other person for his own fancy.

Neutral or indifferent stroke

- Meaning of this is that you are ignoring a person totally and act as if he does not exist.
- You are showing a complete indifference towards that person.
- It is an extremely cruel form of mental punishment.
- You are taking no cognizance of either his being or his doing.

Tips on Giving Strokes

- Be genuine in giving any kind of stroke. Do not fake it.
- Give the stroke for just about a minute. Do not unfold a novel in the praise or criticism of other person. In short, do not overdo.
- Choose the right words, phrases and sentences. It should convey what you wish to say via the stroke you are giving.

- In case of every stroke, let the person know as to why he is receiving that stroke.
- In addition, particularly in case of negative stroke, inform the person where he has made the mistake and guide him on how to correct that mistake.
- Do give the positive stroke in public. Being praised in front of many people boosts the motivation and morale of the recipient.
- But, make sure not to give negative stroke in public. It should be strictly done in privacy. Do not discuss with other what happened between you and the other person whom you gave the stroke.

One More Tip on Strokes: *Stokes' Economy*

It is generally wonderful to give strokes to other people by following strictly the tips given in the earlier paragraph. However, there may be few exceptional situations where you may to economize on giving the strokes (praise or criticism).

If you find that after giving the strokes (praise or criticism), the receiver of the strokes gets disproportionately positively or negatively affected by them you have to put a control on giving the strokes.

What may happen is that because of your positive strokes, the receiver may start feeling falsely elated to the extent that he may become complacent and stop improving himself further. In such a case, you have to give the positive strokes to him with caution and restraint with a subtle or explicit warning not to become complacent after receiving the positive strokes.

Same way, with negative strokes some persons may get disproportionately dejected and may stop performing. There too, as giver of the negative strokes, you may have to ensure that your negative strokes do not harm the receiver in this manner.

Giving and Receiving Praise Help You to Improve Your Life Position

- When you give positive strokes to others, you are recognizing that others are OK too and you become "I am OK, you are OK" from "I am OK, you are not OK". Or if your existing life is "I am OK, you are OK", it further gets strengthened.

- If you are "I am not OK, you are OK" type, receiving praise from others will improve your self-esteem and your OKness about yourself will increase. You then get converted from "I am not OK, you are OK" to "I am OK, you are OK".

Biggest Advantages in Giving and Receiving the Strokes

- They are free of cost.
- They are the simplest yet, the biggest investments in emotional and psychological life of people.
- They are great motivators.
- They improve one's overall personality.
- They increase the emotional bank balances of each other. Refer: *(Emotional Intelligence)* http://emotional-quotient-intelligence.blogspot.com/